LITTLE CLOUD

The Science of a Hurricane

Johanna Wagstaffe

Julie McLaughlin

SCHOLASTIC INC.

Let me tell you a story about a little cloud
that wanted to become a hurricane.

cumulus

nimbostratus

stratus

cirrus

cumulonimbus

altostratus

altocumulus

This little cloud was born just
off the west coast of Africa.

condensation
Warm water makes clouds

evaporation
Water warmed by the sun goes up

Weather Fact
Clouds are made up of billions of little water droplets floating in
the sky. The droplets are so small you can't see them. Some clouds
are high in the sky, and some are closer to the ground. They come
in all shapes and sizes. Clouds get their names on the basis of
where they are in the sky and what they look like.

precipitation
the clouds move over land and cool down, causing rain to fall

runoff
rainwater falls into rivers and runs back into the ocean to start the cycle again!

groundwater

Weather Fact

Like clouds, hurricanes are part of the water cycle. Hurricanes need warm water to grow, so they usually start in tropical places.

Carried by the breeze, the little cloud drifted west toward North America. As it moved over warmer water, it started to get stronger and bigger.

I'm a **cumulus**

Weather Fact

Hurricanes are steered by the winds around them—like the sails on a ship. Those winds can be so strong that they are able to take a hurricane across an ocean.

Weather Fact

Did you know that hurricanes, typhoons and cyclones are all the same kind of storm? They start as clusters of thunderstorms that begin to rotate over tropical waters and are called *tropical cyclones*. What they're eventually called is determined by where in the world they form. Our little cloud will first get classified as a tropical disturbance, then be given a number as he becomes a tropical depression. Next step is tropical storm, and then finally, because he formed in the Atlantic Ocean, he will be called a hurricane. And there are different categories of hurricane strength too.

That strength changed the little cloud. It wasn't just a little cloud anymore. It became a little storm called a tropical depression.

HURRICANE CATEGORIES

CATEGORY 1
74-95 mph winds (120-153 kmh)

It's windy, but most homes won't be damaged.

CATEGORY 2
96-110 mph winds (154-177 kmh)

Getting stronger! Some windows and roofs will see damage.

CATEGORY 3
111-130 mph winds (179-209 kmh)

It's really windy now!
Most homes will see damage.

CATEGORY 4
131-155 mph winds (211-249 kmh)

The wind is so strong now that very
few homes will be able to stay put.

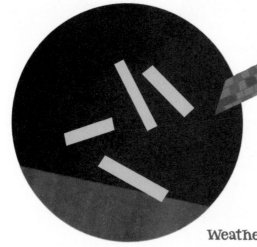

CATEGORY 5
Winds greater than 155 mph (250 kmh)

It's too windy now for homes to stay strong.
Many will be completely destroyed.

Weather Fact

Scientists give storms special names on the basis of the speed of their winds.
Not just any storm gets to be a hurricane. The winds have to be moving at
74 miles (120 kilometers) per hour to be labeled a hurricane. The strongest
hurricane winds travel at more than 186 miles (300 kilometers) per hour.

As the tropical depression moved along, it got even stronger and changed again, becoming a tropical storm. Something very special happened to the little storm then. Scientists gave it a name—Nate. The little storm had always wanted a name.

Weather Fact

Every strong tropical cyclone gets its own name. That's important, because there can be more than one storm in the world at the same time. It avoids confusion when scientists are warning people about a storm coming their way. Imagine if everyone in your class had the same name!

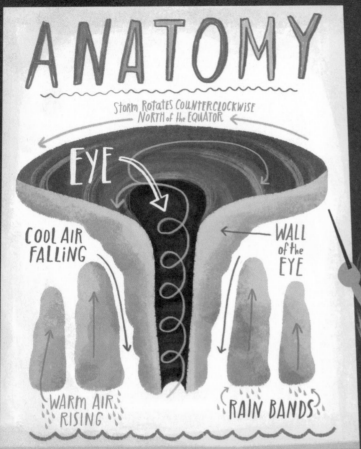

ANATOMY

STORM ROTATES COUNTERCLOCKWISE NORTH of the EQUATOR

EYE

COOL AIR FALLING

WALL of the EYE

WARM AIR RISING

RAIN BANDS

Finally Nate's winds were strong enough that he became a full hurricane! He loved his spinning winds and towering clouds, but his favorite part was his eye.

Weather Fact

The eye of a hurricane is the center of the storm. It's very calm there—blue sky, birds chirping. The rest of the storm spins around the eye. The strongest winds are beside the eye.

As Nate moved across the water, he saw something in the distance—he was getting closer to land. And to all the people and their homes on that land. The people were already talking about Nate and getting ready for his arrival.

Weather Fact

Scientists try to predict when and where a hurricane will reach land and how strong the winds will be. Scientists and officials issue a series of weather warnings before the storm arrives to help people prepare and stay safe.

They were hoping that Nate would miss them...

...but just in case, they prepared for Nate. Nate couldn't slow down or change course on his own, but he didn't want to scare the people down below!

Weather Fact

Scientists are able to make predictions about hurricanes several days in advance. Their forecast gets better as the storm gets closer. They look at satellite pictures of the storm from space and measure temperature and winds, using instruments attached to buoys or to balloons high up in the sky. There are even special planes that can fly right into the storm.

Scientists then tell emergency officials what to expect so they can start preparing people. Sometimes this means telling people to stock up on water and supplies in case the power goes out. Or it could mean canceling events so that people stay indoors. Sometimes it means asking people to leave their homes and go somewhere safer.

The job of reporters is to make sure everyone is getting the right message.

As Nate got closer to the land, he realized he would roll over the tall mountains along the coast before he made landfall. And as he moved away from the warm water, he began to weaken. He could feel the tops of the mountains starting to slow him down.

Weather Fact

A slow hurricane might sound like a good thing. But slow refers to how fast the storm is moving forward, not how strong its winds are. Slow storms are the most dangerous kind because they bring strong winds and rain to one area for a long time. If a hurricane hits a mountain and slows down over the peaks, communities on the other side will be spared the worst of the storm.

Nate slowed down so much, in fact, that he almost stopped. All the warm air that had churned inside him and given him strength turned into raindrops that flowed out of him.

Weather Fact

Hurricanes are known for their heavy rain and strong winds. These winds act like a bulldozer, pushing ocean water ahead of the storm. When this mound of water gets to the coastline, it can create dangerous flooding called *storm surge*. Even the very edges of a spinning hurricane can create thunderstorms and tornadoes!

And just like that, having lost his strength, Nate was a tropical depression again. The people on land were still watching him, but they were relieved that Nate had changed from a hurricane into a much weaker storm.

Weather Fact

As technology improves, forecasters will make better hurricane predictions. New satellites going into space will help track storms with more accuracy than ever before. Computers are getting faster and more powerful at correctly determining what directions storms might take.

Even though he never made it to land as a hurricane, the little cloud still managed to cause a lot of problems. As he drifted northward and became just a few water droplets once again, the little cloud wondered what his next adventure would be and hoped that, whatever it was, he could bring some good weather to people instead.

Weather Fact

Did you know that every drop of water on our planet has been recycling itself for four billion years?

FACT PAGE

- The World Meteorological Organization assigns names to storms. It creates a list of names, starting with the letter *A* and continuing through to the letter *Z*, for each of six years and then rotates them. But if a certain hurricane is really destructive, its name will be retired forever. Until 1978, hurricanes had only female names, such as Carol, Hazel and Edna. Now names are male and female.

- Did you know that storms north of the equator rotate counterclockwise and storms south of the equator rotate clockwise? That's because of how the earth rotates.

- The east coast of North America usually gets about seven hurricanes every four years.

- One of the most well-known hurricanes is Hurricane Katrina, which killed more than 1,800 people in the United States and caused more than $150 billion in damage. The city of New Orleans was hit particularly hard—80 percent of the city was flooded.

- Because hurricanes need warm water to form, there is an official beginning and end to a hurricane season. In the Atlantic Ocean the season runs from about June 1 to November 30. For the waters around North and Central America, the season officially begins on May 15 and ends November 30. Of course, storms can form before or after the usual time frame.

- Humans are changing the climate of the planet. Because temperatures are increasing, ice is melting and oceans are rising. This means higher storm surge, more rain and more fuel for our hurricanes. So scientists need your help to learn as much as you can about the world around you. The more understanding you have about storms, the more changes you can make. Who knows, maybe you'll even help save an entire city from a hurricane one day!

Johanna

ALERT!! HURRICANE WARNING!

AUTHOR'S NOTE

Hurricanes, tornadoes, flooding, blizzards—the list goes on. Severe weather can be a fascinating force of nature. In fact, my favorite classes when I was a student were the ones about destructive weather. How can the skies that give us the perfect beach day or a magical winter morning be the same skies that create a hurricane with winds so strong they can knock down trees?

It was this curiosity that started me off on my journey to become a *meteorologist*. I use science to figure out what the weather will be like before you head out for the day. And I also forecast severe weather—like hurricanes—that might be dangerous to a lot of people.

In 2018 I was sent to Florida to report on a hurricane for the first time. Hurricane Irma was a category 5 storm, and it looked like it was headed straight for the east coast. It was scary to feel the winds picking up in strength. We were evacuated from our hotel because of the approaching storm. In the end we were spared the worst of it, but I experienced hurricane winds so strong I could barely stand. Luckily, I had a whole team helping to keep me safe so that I could tell people where the worst winds would be.

Just like Nate, I would rather have good weather to tell people about, but I like knowing I can help people stay safe.

To my own little cloud and all the adventures that lie ahead.
—J.W.

For my family, my partner and my furricane, Mr. Pants.
—J.M.

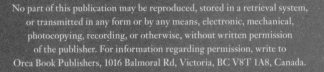

ISBN 978-1-338-65205-5

Text copyright © 2020 by Johanna Wagstaffe. Illustrations copyright © 2020 by Julie McLaughlin. All rights reserved. Published by Scholastic Inc., 557 Broadway, New York, NY 10012, by arrangement with Orca Book Publishers. SCHOLASTIC and associated logos are trademarks and/or registered trademarks of Scholastic Inc.

12 11 10 9 8 7 6 5 4 3 2   21 22 23 24 25

Printed in the U.S.A.   40

First Scholastic printing, January 2020

Artwork created with graphite and finished digitally
Author photo by CBC
Cover and interior artwork by Julie McLaughlin
Design by Rachel Page and Julie McLaughlin